START

ACING INTERVIEWS

NOW!

A Proven System for Effectively Answering Interview Questions

Kurt Thompson

The Interview Pro

www.theinterviewpro.com

ISBN- 1453749608
ISBN-13: 9781453749609
www.theinterviewpro.com

Disclaimer and Terms of Use: No information contained in this book should be considered as financial, tax, or legal advice. Your reliance upon information and content obtained by you at or through this publication is solely at your own risk. The author assumes no liability or responsibility for damage or injury to you, other persons, or property arising from any use of any product, information, idea, or instruction contained in the content or services provided to you through this book. Reliance upon information contained in this material is solely at the reader's own risk.

Foreword

"The job does not go to the most qualified candidate; the job goes to the best interviewer."

My name is Kurt Thompson – The Interview Pro. I have been a hiring manager since 1996, with much of that time spent at a Human Resource consulting company. I have interviewed hundreds of potential job candidates. I'd love to say that all have come fully prepared for the interview. However, the reality is few are ready for one of the most important meetings in their life.

I have noticed that many people spend a great deal of time and money perfecting their resumes, but very little time perfecting their interviewing skills. **The resume may get you the interview, but it is the interview that gets you the job.**

As an interviewer, it's hard to watch a candidate struggle to answer questions and veer off on a tangent, or not really know how to answer a question at all. It's even worse when you know the person is highly qualified for the job. I have come to the conclusion that most candidates simply do not know what to expect during the interview process. Therefore, they cannot really be prepared.

This experience inspired me to begin interview coaching. Over the years I've coached countless individuals on how to prepare for a variety of job interviews. My clients' backgrounds range from a high school education, to recent college graduates, to those with 20+ years of senior-level professional experience. As an interview coach, I have conducted group interview coaching seminars, as well as individual consultations.

During this time, I developed the **START Method** for answering job interview questions. It's been proven to help candidates from a variety of backgrounds be prepared to effectively and confidently answer the majority of questions they face in an interview.

The START Method for answering interview questions helps my clients to better prepare for their interviews, and have much more confidence going into their interviews. The START Method enables them to effectively answer interview questions to best showcase their talents and experiences, thus putting them in a position to get the job they desire.

I hope this workbook helps you to gain the skills and confidence to effectively answer the interview questions you will face and ultimately lead you to land the job that you desire.

Kurt Thompson – The Interview Pro

Introduction

There are so many aspects to the interview process; it can be quite overwhelming to know exactly how to prepare. From developing your resume and references; to researching the company you are meeting; to anticipating the questions you are asked and how to answer them—not to mention developing a list of questions to ask; and your follow-up strategies.

To compound the issue, the skills required to interview effectively may lie dormant for years. Most people stay in the same job for several years, so there is no reason to keep these skills sharp. However, when you are in a job search, these interviewing skills are critical to your success. Overnight, you need to instantly become an interviewing expert.

Interviews can take on many forms: telephone screens, first interviews, second interviews, group interviews, panel interviews, etc. Regardless of the format of the interview, you'll find that about 75 to 80% of your time during the interview is spent answering a series of questions about your background, professional skills and experiences. How well you answer these questions greatly determines whether or not you are offered the job.

This is where most interviewees trip up. They don't adequately anticipate the questions, or think about the most effective way to answer those questions. In many cases the interviewees have not taken enough time to reflect on their accomplishments or chosen the right "success stories" to build their interview answers.

The irony is that most interview questions can be anticipated, and the interviewers have been *conditioned to hear* the questions answered in a certain manner. Once you realize and understand this, answering interview questions will be like taking a test where you not only know what questions will be asked, but the answers as well!

The goal of this workbook is to demystify the interview process. After using the tools in this workbook you will be able to clearly and effectively answer nearly any interview question you are asked. This knowledge and preparation will give you the confidence to succeed in the interview and land the job that you desire.

The interview may be the most important meeting of your life. You cannot be too prepared. Being properly prepared for an interview gives you an advantage.

START Method for Acing Job Interview Questions Workbook

How to Use this Workbook

The primary purpose of this workbook is to help you prepare for the question and answer portion of the interview. While this workbook is not broken down into specific chapters, there are four basic components:

1) An overview of Behavior-Based interview questions.

2) The introduction of the START Method for answering interview questions.

3) An identification of the ten most common categories of interview questions, as well as specific examples of the most common interview questions in each category.

4) The START worksheets – use them to build your personal START answers.

You will also find additional information and resources at the end of this workbook.

After reviewing the information on behavior-based interview questions and the START Method for answering interview questions, take your time looking through the examples of the common interview questions. Think about the positions you are interviewing for and identify the questions you are most likely to be asked. If you have a job description for the position, use it to help you formulate the questions you will face.

Select one or two questions from each category to prepare for. If you want to challenge yourself, choose a question that you feel uncomfortable answering.

After you select the questions, use the included START worksheets to write out your answers. Do not use the first situation that comes into your mind to build your answer. Rather, challenge yourself to think about an experience that would best showcase your talents and expertise. Many times the first situation you think of will not be your best choice.

As a goal, I recommend that you develop eight to ten strong START answers that you are comfortable using in an interview. This number of well-prepared "success stories" will place you well ahead of your competition. A well-defined START answer will help you demonstrate your unique skills and experience in almost any interview.

There are eight START worksheets in this workbook. If you need more, simply make additional copies or download them from www.theinterviewpro.com.

Behavior-Based Interview

The most common type of interview is called "behavior-based". The theory of behavior-based interviews is that your past performance is a leading indicator of future behavior. This style has been an accepted practice in larger organizations for several years. However, this approach has become increasingly common in smaller companies too.

In this type of interview, the questions are designed to see how you have handled similar situations *in the past*. In a behavior-based interview, the interviewer will ask questions that help him to understand two things:

1) Situations, projects or problems that you have encountered in previous experiences.
2) How you have specifically dealt with a situation in the past.

Behavior-based questions typically start with "Tell me about a time…", or "Describe a time when…" The questions are structured so that you answer with details of a specific experience you've encountered—and how you handled it. The interviewer is not looking for a general "What you would do" if such a situation were to occur. The focus of this type of interview is on your *specific accomplishments and experiences*, and less on your thoughts about how you might handle such a situation.

Professional interviewers who are trained in behavioral-based interviewing are conditioned to hear answers structured in a very specific way. This involves looking for answers that are based on a specific past experience and have a clear beginning, middle and end to the story.

Interestingly, if an interviewer asks the same question of two candidates, and each gives the same answer; except that the first candidate answers in a manner consistent with the interviewer's training and the second does not; the interviewer will conclude that the first candidate answered the question better, and is the better candidate.

The key to successfully answering behavior-based interview questions is to understand "how" the interviewer has been trained to hear the answers. With this knowledge, you can prepare specific examples of the types of situations you have faced in your work experience.

The START Method for answering interview questions will help you answer behavior-based interview questions in the most effective manner possible.

What is The START Method?

The START Method is a technique that helps you craft replies to behavior-based interview questions in a manner that provides the interviewer with a clear answer. Answers structured in this manner resonate with the interviewer who is trained to ask such questions. This is how trained interviewers have been conditioned to listen to interview answers.

START is an acronym for:

- **S/T - S**ITUATION **or T**ASK

- **A - A**CTION

- **R - R**ESULT

- **T - T**AKE AWAY

The ability to tell a good story helps you to communicate more effectively. This is especially true in an interview setting. When you successfully convey your story in an interview, you are able to effectively communicate your key skills, talents and experiences. In doing so, you are more likely to be perceived as the best candidate for the job.

The key to telling a good story is to have a clear beginning, middle and end. This is true of interview answers as well. A common mistake that candidates make is to ramble and not have a clear flow to their answer. Actually, another common mistake is just the opposite. Some applicants do not offer enough detail for the hiring manager to get a clear picture of their talents and experience.

This is how the START Method will greatly assist you. Answering questions with this method will help you *tell a memorable story* that enables the interviewer to fully grasp your professional capabilities, strengths and experiences. By learning this simple yet powerful technique, you can provide clear answers with just the right amount of detail and provide the interviewer with the information she needs.

The candidate who best paints a picture of success in the interviewer's mind has an advantage over other applicants. It's the ability to tell a mini-story that will make you a more successful interviewer. The START Method helps you do just that.

Once the question is posed by the interviewer, use the START Method to structure your answer as follows:

SITUATION or TASK: Describe a specific situation you have faced or a task that was assigned to you. The situation may also be described as a problem or an obstacle. Think of this as the beginning, or the set-up, of the short story you are about to tell.

ACTION: Describe the action (or activity) you took to address the situation described above. Include the specific skills, strengths or attributes that you used.

RESULTS: Talk about the favorable outcomes that directly resulted from your actions. Your story will be more powerful when you can describe specific and measurable results.

TAKE AWAY: Identify what you learned from the experience, what you were able to "take away" from the experience, or how the experience helped you grow and develop as a professional. You can also describe how you applied the experience to other situations. Adding a take-away to your answer will bring your story to a nice close. Think of the take-away as the summary of the story you have just told.

Remember that answering questions within this structure will increase your ability to *stay on track*. You will also more clearly articulate your answer in a way that helps the interviewer to follow, understand and remember what you say.

The good news is nearly 90% of interview questions can be answered using the START Method. Once you learn this easy-to-use technique, you will answer interview questions much more confidently and effectively.

There are examples of answers to real-life interview questions using the START Method on the following pages. Use these examples to understand how to use the START Method before you work on your own answers.

Question and Answer Example #1:

Question: "Tell me about a time you had to deal with an angry customer?"

Answer: "After a long sales process, one of my sales consultants closed a large account. When the client received their first invoice, they called customer service and said that the agreed upon rates were not reflected in the invoice. Our customer service department contacted me.

I immediately called the client to better understand their concerns. As it turned out, there was a misunderstanding regarding the rate structure. The client was pretty upset about this and implied that they were misled by the sales rep. I listened to their concerns and took as many notes as I could. It was clear to me that this would not be resolved over the phone, so I asked for a face-to-face meeting. Prior to the meeting, I reviewed the proposal in detail and saw some items that were not as clear as they could have been. I also saw items that the client misinterpreted.

When I got to the meeting the client was still pretty upset. But I was well prepared to walk them through their concerns one by one. As it turned out, we did have to make some concessions. But there were some areas where we were able to hold our ground. After we met, the client was satisfied with the resolution and is still a satisfied client today.

I learned from this experience that it's best to address issues head on. It wasn't comfortable pushing for a meeting when I knew I was heading into a hostile environment. However, sitting down with the parties involved allowed me to have a better dialogue with them to get to a resolution quickly."

In example #1, here is how the START Method was used:

- The **SITUATION or TASK (ST)** is a client who is upset upon reviewing their first invoice.

- The **ACTION (A)** is to immediately contact the client, schedule a face-to-face meeting, research the issue and identify potential solutions prior to the meeting.

- The **RESULT (R)** is a satisfied client.

- The **TAKE AWAY (T)** is learning to address sensitive issues head on, and if possible, in a face-to-face environment.

Question and Answer Example #2:

Question: "Describe a complex project that you successfully managed."

Answer: "As an analyst for a financial institution working with 401(k) providers, I managed the "unclaimed check" program. This involved uncashed 401(k) distribution checks sent to participants.

A new Department of Labor regulation impacted our current process and many of the departments within our company. To make matters worse, the deadline set by the DOL was very tight. I was tasked with heading up the transition and compliance as a result of the changes.

Many of our departments were affected. There were Client Managers who worked with the 401(k) providers, the 401(k) providers themselves, the plan sponsors and participants. Also, there were our internal training, compliance and IT departments.

After mapping out a transition plan, I realized that each entity had their own set of needs and they had to be communicated with in different ways. I created specific training and communications for each department so they knew how the changes affected their responsibilities and processes.

Finally, I worked through the testing process with our IT department to ensure the changes followed our internal processes and remained in compliance with the new regulations.

In the end, we were able to complete the project three weeks prior to the deadline. This allowed our clients, the plan sponsors, to earn interest on the uncashed checks even earlier. As a result of successfully overseeing this project, I was awarded the Employee of the Quarter honor.

I learned that it is important to recognize that communication needs vary from department to department when dealing with large-scale change. Listening to the needs of each group and tailoring messages for them made a large impact on the success of the project."

In example #2, here is how the START Method was used:

- The **SITUATION or TASK (ST)** is a 401(k) regulation change that resulted in a new project.

- The **ACTION (A)** is the prioritization and customization of the communication rollout.

- The **RESULT (R)** is successfully completing the project before the deadline.

- The **TAKE AWAY (T)** is the importance of responding to different communication styles.

Question and Answer Example #3:

Question: "Tell me about a time you had to use your creativity to solve a problem."

Answer: "My company handled the warranty return and exchange of cell phone equipment for the customers of a major carrier. In my role as Program Manager of Equipment Exchange, I oversaw the actual exchange and return of the equipment.

When customers had a defective phone, they contacted us and we shipped out a replacement phone along with a package for the customer to return the defective phone.

Unfortunately, we had a rather labor-intensive process to verify that we received the right equipment from the customer. This involved manually cross-referencing the phone we received in both our system and the carrier's system. Problems frequently occurred when customers sent us different equipment than the phone they received in the exchange program. When this happened, the customer would continue to receive a charge on their monthly bill. Of course, this resulted in customer issues and resulted in customer service complaints to our client, the carrier.

I came up with the idea of placing a bar coded sticker on the inside of the return package. The bar code contained the customer billing and equipment information.

I worked with our IT department to create a bar code sticker that would interface both with our system and the carrier's system. I also coordinated with our Shipping and Handling department to ensure that each return would be scanned as soon as they were received.

In the end, this improvement resulted in quite a few benefits. Since we could verify the returned equipment much faster, this significantly decreased the number of times the customer would receive a billing charge. If there were any issues with the returned phone, we were able to quickly investigate. Also, the carrier was notified that items had been returned on average two days faster because we did not have to manually verify each return.

Having gone through this experience, I learned that there is always room for improvement. I also learned that it is okay to challenge the status quo. Just because we have been doing something one way for awhile, there still may be a better way."

Here is how the START Method was used in example #3:

- The **SITUATION or TASK (ST)** is the customer service problems that resulted from the manual verification process for the returned equipment.

- The **ACTION (A)** is the idea for the bar code sticker inside the return packaging and the subsequent coordination between the departments and the client to make sure the new process worked.

- The **RESULT (R)** is reduced billing errors and increased customer satisfaction. There was also considerable time savings by the company and the client as a result of the new process.

- The **TAKE AWAY (T)** is that it is good to challenge the current way of doing things, and there is always room for improvement.

In each example, the START Method is used to answer the interview question with a mini-story that has a clearly-defined beginning, middle and end. This structure makes it easier for the listener to follow and understand the answer. The START Method also helps keep the response succinct and avoids long, rambling answers.

When hiring managers are trained in behavior-based interviewing, they are conditioned to listen for answers that are constructed in the manner that the START Method provides. When you answer interview questions this way, you are "speaking the language" of the interviewer. By using the START Method as the examples show, you will communicate with the interviewer in a way that they have been trained and conditioned to communicate during an interview.

Preparing to ACE Interview Questions

Before you begin work on preparing for your interview, let me provide you with a simple 3 step process to help you ACE your interview questions.

A – Anticipate: Before you start working on your answers for your interviews, you must properly anticipate the questions you will most likely be asked. Failure to do so may result in either spending time or energy preparing for questions you will not be asked, or failing to prepare for questions you will encounter. The good news is that most interview questions can be easily anticipated. In the next section of this book I have identified many of the most common interview questions.

If you are preparing for a specific job interview, try to obtain a job description for the position you will be interviewing for. You may able to obtain a job description from the person you will be meeting with, or from the company's human resource department. Another way to acquire a job description is from the company's website.

If you are unable to get a job description from the company for the position you are interviewing for, search the internet for job descriptions for similar positions at other companies. (Monster.com and CareerBuilder.com are good resources). If you are not preparing for a specific interview, seek out job descriptions for positions you will be applying for.

Another avenue for job descriptions is by talking to people who currently hold a job similar to the one you are seeking. If you know someone in this position, ask for an informational interview to gain a better understanding of the requirements of the position. If you do not know someone directly, by networking you may be able to identify a candidate for an informational interview.

Once you have a job description, carefully review the background, requirements and desired skills for the position. Think about the questions you would ask if you were the interviewer to determine the qualifications of a candidate. Use the interview questions I have outlined in the next section to help with this task. Make it a goal to create a list of 10-12 potential interview questions you believe will be asked.

C – Customize Your Answer: Now that you have anticipated and created a list of interview questions, you need to prepare and customize your answers. As you start reviewing your list of interview questions, you will probably realize that there is more than one way to answer each question.

Let's say that you didn't prepare in advance of the interview – once you were asked a question in the interview you would have about 5-10 seconds to begin your answer – not much time. With such short lead time you probably would not choose the best answer. The good news is that when you prepare in advance of the interview you can choose the best way to answer each question.

As part of the preparation process it is important to reflect on your experiences, accomplishments, milestones, setbacks and failures. Take a good hard look at your resume and reflect on your career and the positions that you have held.

Review your list of questions and start thinking of the experiences, examples and anecdotes that would best answer the question. Once you have identified the experiences you are going to use to formulate your answers, the next step is HOW to best answer the question. This is where the START Method comes into play. Use the START Worksheets in this book to help write out your answers.

E – Execute: Now that you have anticipated your questions and customized your answers, you have the basis of a game plan to ace your interview questions. Now the key is to execute.

To execute at the highest level, you need to practice. Interviewing is a skill – and like any skill it can be developed. The key to developing any skill is to practice. The same is true of interview skills.

The best way to develop interviewing skills is through a mock interview. A mock interview will allow you to go through a simulated interview to rehearse and refine your interview answers. I recommend the services of a professional interview coach or a career counselor. The opportunity to practice your interview skills with professional feedback will give you the confidence that will enable you to excel in a real interview.

If you are unable to find professional services that fit your needs, enlist the services of a trusted advisor who can help you with a mock interview. A trusted advisor may be a professional acquaintance, friend, relative or spouse

The Question and Answer Session

The heart of the interview process is the question and answer session. The interviewer is trying to determine how well your experiences, skills and attributes match up with the position that is to be filled.

Many times the interviewer has a set of prepared questions. Other times, the interviewer uses your resume or application as an interview guide. Some interviewers may just ask questions in a casual or conversational way.

The most common interview questions can be grouped into ten categories:

1) General Job-Related
2) Communications
3) Motivation/Self-Starter
4) Results-Oriented
5) Team Player
6) Problem-Solving
7) Leadership
8) Organization
9) Resiliency
10) Miscellaneous

The following lists of questions are not intended to represent the only questions asked in an interview. On each page, there is space for you to identify questions that you may face in your interviews. For certain jobs, there are industry-specific interview questions.

Choose the questions you think you're most likely to encounter in your upcoming interviews and build your own answers using the START Method. At the end of this section are START worksheets to build your answers.

You may choose to create more worksheets for yourself, or download additional worksheets from www.theinterviewpro.com. Before you begin using the worksheets, review page 24 for how to best use the START worksheets.

Type 1: General Job-Related Questions

These questions help the interviewer get a general idea of the kinds of positions you've held, the types of companies and people you've worked with, and your past roles and responsibilities.

- Tell me about the last position (or positions) you held.
- Describe the company (or companies) that you've worked for.
- What did you like *most* about your last job?
- What did you like *least* about your last job?
- What is the most important thing you learned in your last position?
- What would your supervisor say about you?
- What attracted you to your last position (or positions)?
- Why did you leave your last position (or positions)?
- Tell me about your favorite boss.
- Tell me about your *least* favorite boss.
- What does work/life balance mean to you?
- Explain the gaps in your employment (if applicable).

Develop additional general job-related questions you may encounter:

1) _____

_____

2) _____

_____

3) _____

_____

4) _____

_____

Type 2: Communication

The following questions are designed to assess the strength of the candidate's *communication* skills and experiences.

- Tell me about a time when you had to deliver a group presentation.
- Describe a time when you had to deliver a tough message.
- Tell me about a time when you had to persuade someone to your point of view.
- Tell me about a time when you disagreed with a supervisor or coworker. How did you handle the situation?
- Describe a time when you had to use excellent communication skills.
- Have you ever had to adjust your personal style of communication to adapt to someone else's style of communication?
- Describe a critical written document that you had to create.
- What is your preferred style of communication – phone or email?

Develop additional communication skills questions you may encounter:

1) _____

_____

2) _____

_____

3) _____

_____

4) _____

_____

Type 3: Motivation/Self Starter

An interviewer will ask these types of questions to assess motivation and self-starter attributes the candidate may possess.

- Where do you see yourself in 5 years?
- What are you passionate about?
- What motivates you?
- How do you keep yourself going during difficult times?
- What have you done to keep yourself current in your profession?
- What are you looking for in your next position?
- What professional goals do you have for yourself—and how do you know you're on track to achieve them?
- What are your career goals?

Develop additional motivation/self-starter skills questions you may encounter:

1) _____

_____

2) _____

_____

3) _____

_____

4) _____

_____

Type 4: Results-Oriented

The following questions are designed to see if a candidate is results-oriented.

- What is your greatest career accomplishment?
- What were the expectations in your last position and how did you achieve them?
- What are you most proud of in your career?
- What have you done to help your company increase revenue?
- What have you done to help your company reduce expenses?
- What have you done to help your company become more efficient?
- Do you consider yourself to be successful? Why?
- Describe a time when you went the "extra mile" to get the job done.
- How have you added value to your job over time?

Develop additional results-oriented questions you may encounter:

1) _____

_____

2) _____

_____

3) _____

_____

4) _____

_____

Type 5: Team Player

The following are commonly-asked questions to assess whether a candidate is a team player.

- Describe a time when you worked on a group project.
- What type of personalities do you find it most difficult to work with?
- What type of personalities do you enjoy working with the most?
- Do you prefer to work by yourself or with others?
- Describe a time when you recognized the efforts or results of a coworker.
- Describe a time when you disagreed with a coworker or supervisor.
- Have you ever had to make a decision that affected you negatively, but impacted others positively?

Develop additional team player questions you may encounter:

1) _____

_____

2) _____

_____

3) _____

_____

4) _____

_____

Type 6: Problem-Solving

With more emphasis being put on workplace productivity, candidates who demonstrate problem-solving skills are increasingly sought after.

- Describe a difficult problem or situation you recently dealt with. How did you overcome it?
- Tell me about a challenge that you have faced in your last position.
- Describe a difficult time or situation at work. What did you do?
- Describe a creative approach you have taken to solve a problem at work.
- Have you ever had to resolve an issue or dispute between two or more people?
- What is the best work idea that you have come up with?
- Describe a time that you made a wrong decision. How did you handle it?
- Have you ever had to deal with an angry customer or client?

Develop additional problem-solving questions you may encounter:

1) _____

_____

2) _____

_____

3) _____

_____

4) _____

_____

Type 7: Leadership

Of course, assessing leadership skills is critical when interviewing candidates for management positions. However, these skills are also important for non-managers.

- Describe your leadership style.
- Tell me about a time you had a leadership role in a group project.
- Describe a time when you had to lead a group of people that did not report directly to you.
- Describe a time you had to motivate a team or an individual.
- What do you look for when you hire someone?
- What does leadership mean to you?
- Have you ever had to fire someone? How did you handle it?
- Talk about a time you faced a difficult leadership situation.
- How many people have you managed?
- Have you ever had to manage remote located employees?
- How would your direct reports describe your leadership style?

Develop additional leadership questions you may encounter:

1) _____

_____

2) _____

_____

3) _____

_____

4) _____

_____

Type 8: Organization and Time Management

Nearly every interviewer will include a question to assess the organization and time-management skills of the candidate.

- Describe a time when your workload was heavy and you were able to handle it.
- Describe a complex project that you successfully managed.
- Describe your time management system.
- How do you keep yourself organized?
- Tell me about a time when you had to deal with conflicting demands.
- Describe a time when you had too many things do and you had to prioritize your tasks.
- Describe a time when you had to accomplish a great deal of work in a short period of time?
- If there was only enough time to finish one of two critical projects, how would you decide which one to complete?
- Are you able to multi-task?

Develop additional organization and time-management questions you may encounter:

1) _____

_____

2) _____

_____

3) _____

_____

4) _____

_____

Type 9: Resiliency

Interviewers commonly want to know how resilient a candidate is in a variety of situations (often, negative).

- Tell me about a time when you fell short of expectations. What happened?
- Tell me about a job that did not work out.
- Tell me about a time when you have failed.
- Describe a time when you had to deal with major change at work.
- Describe a time when you had what you thought to be a great idea at work only to have the idea rejected.
- Do you feel you have ever been unfairly criticized?
- Have you ever been fired?
- What is your greatest weakness?
- What has been your biggest professional disappointment?
- How do you handle stress or pressure at work?
- If you are not offered this position, what will you do?

Develop additional resiliency questions you may encounter:

1) _____

_____

2) _____

_____

3) _____

_____

4) _____

_____

Type 10: Miscellaneous

The following are examples of miscellaneous questions you may encounter in an interview.

- What interests you about this position/company?
- How did you prepare for this interview?
- What is your ideal job?
- What do you know about our company?
- What type of work hours do you prefer?
- Do you ever take work home?
- What does work/life balance mean to you?

Develop additional organization and time management questions you may encounter:

1) _____

_____

2) _____

_____

3) _____

_____

4) _____

_____

How to Use the START Worksheets

- Thoroughly review your resume before beginning to work on your answers. Challenge yourself to reflect on your career and accomplishments. Try to remember your accomplishments and the problems you have encountered. This will help you identify the areas of your career and experience to build your answers around.

- Choose eight to ten questions you are most likely to encounter in your interviews. If you really want to challenge yourself, work on questions that you would have the most difficulty answering in an interview.

- Using the START worksheets, write out the **Situation (S)**. For the first draft, simply brainstorm and write what you can recall of the events. Do the same thing for the **Action (A)** you took, the **Result (R)** and the **Take Away (T)**.

- Once you have completed the first draft, go back and edit it. When you have an answer that you like, read it out loud (preferably to someone else). Make sure that you're happy with the way the words sound. The answer should be one to two minutes in length.

- Set a goal to develop at least eight START answers. Don't try to memorize the answers verbatim. Rather, have a good grasp of the essence of each answer. Make sure you have internalized the answer well enough so that you can answer each question in a conversational manner.

- Once you have developed your answers using the START worksheets, you may notice that the answer for one question will also work to answer other questions as well. For example, the answer to a question regarding managing a complex project may easily apply to questions on time management, use of communication skills, effective leadership, etc. Do not feel you have to lock-in one answer for a specific question.

- If you need more START worksheets, download them from www.theinterviewpro.com.

START Worksheet

Choose a question that you want to prepare for an interview. Think of a strong example from your experience and use the worksheet to formulate your START answer.

Question:

_____

_____

Situation or Task (ST):

_____

_____

_____

_____

Action (A):

_____

_____

_____

_____

Result (R):

_____

_____

Take Away (T):

_____

_____

START Worksheet

Choose a question that you want to prepare for an interview. Think of a strong example from your experience and use the worksheet to formulate your START answer.

Question:

_____

_____

Situation or Task (ST):

_____

_____

_____

_____

Action (A):

_____

_____

_____

_____

Result (R):

_____

_____

Take Away (T):

_____

_____

START Worksheet

Choose a question that you want to prepare for an interview. Think of a strong example from your experience and use the worksheet to formulate your START answer.

Question:

_____

_____

Situation or Task (ST):

_____

_____

_____

_____

Action (A):

_____

_____

_____

_____

Result (R):

_____

_____

Take Away (T):

_____

_____

START Worksheet

Choose a question that you want to prepare for an interview. Think of a strong example from your experience and use the worksheet to formulate your START answer.

Question:

_____

_____

Situation or Task (ST):

_____

_____

_____

_____

Action (A):

_____

_____

_____

_____

Result (R):

_____

_____

Take Away (T):

_____

_____

START Worksheet

Choose a question that you want to prepare for an interview. Think of a strong example from your experience and use the worksheet to formulate your START answer.

Question:

_____

_____

Situation or Task (ST):

_____

_____

_____

_____

Action (A):

_____

_____

_____

_____

Result (R):

_____

_____

Take Away (T):

_____

_____

START Worksheet

Choose a question that you want to prepare for an interview. Think of a strong example from your experience and use the worksheet to formulate your START answer.

Question:

_____

_____

Situation or Task (ST):

_____

_____

_____

_____

Action (A):

_____

_____

_____

_____

Result (R):

_____

_____

Take Away (T):

_____

_____

START Worksheet

Choose a question that you want to prepare for an interview. Think of a strong example from your experience and use the worksheet to formulate your START answer.

Question:

_____

_____

Situation or Task (ST):

_____

_____

_____

_____

Action (A):

_____

_____

_____

_____

Result (R):

_____

_____

Take Away (T):

_____

_____

START Worksheet

Choose a question that you want to prepare for an interview. Think of a strong example from your experience and use the worksheet to formulate your START answer.

Question:

_____

_____

Situation or Task (ST):

_____

_____

_____

_____

Action (A):

_____

_____

_____

_____

Result (R):

_____

_____

Take Away (T):

_____

_____

Other Types of Interview Questions

While behavior-based interview questions are certainly the most prevalent, there are other types of interview questions you may encounter. The most common are:

1) Skills-based questions.

2) Experience-based questions.

Skills-based questions help the interviewer learn if you have a basic *skill* that is necessary for the job. The question may be as simple as:

- "Are you proficient at Microsoft Excel?"

- "How many words can you type per minute?"

Experience-based questions enable the interviewer to understand how much relevant experience you have, or if you have a background in an area deemed important for the job. Examples of experience-based questions would be:

- "Have you ever had experience dealing with customers over the phone?"

- "How much experience have you had dealing with purchasing agents?"

The challenge with these types of questions is that they lend themselves to short "yes" or "no" type answers. Many times, the interviewee falls into the trap of providing a short, non-impactful answer. While it may seem that you are answering the question appropriately, your answer does not enable the interviewer to get a good grasp of your capabilities and experiences.

Use the START Method to answer these types of questions much more effectively. An answer for "Are you proficient at Microsoft Excel?" might be, "Yes, I am very proficient at Excel. I used Excel in each of my past three positions, covering the past nine years." It seems that you've answered the question well enough. After all, the interviewer wanted to know if you have the experience they're looking for, and the answer was 'yes'.

However, by using the START Method you will provide a much more impactful answer.

This is how the same question can be answered using the START Method.

<u>Question</u>: "Are you proficient at Microsoft Excel?"

<u>Answer:</u> "Why, yes, I am very adept at Excel. Recently, my supervisor asked me to compile a revised market sales forecast that needed to be turned around quickly.

I assembled the individual sales forecasts from each of the Regional Managers. Once I did that, I created a spreadsheet with formulas that calculated the sum of all the forecasts. I also created another formula to show the percentage of budget for each area.

While it wasn't part of the request, I also created a few graphs and charts to go along with the forecast. In the end, I was able to finish the forecast in the timeframe requested. My boss especially liked the added graphs and charts. I realize that being skilled in Excel is important. I make a point of staying current by taking occasional courses in Excel."

It would have been easy to provide a short answer. However, the START Method will help you answer these types of questions in a more impactful and comprehensive way.

The same method can be used for experience-based questions. For example, if this question had been asked "So, how much experience have you had working with Microsoft Excel?", you can answer by telling the interviewer how many years of experience you've had with Excel, and then add the START example to help the interviewer understand the type of work you have done in this area.

The key is to avoid short, vague answers. This type of answer doesn't help the interviewer create a strong mental image of your strengths and experiences. Regardless of the type of questions, by using the START Method you'll not simply answer questions; you'll be able to tell concise stories that truly describe your skills, experiences and capabilities.

ADDITIONAL RESOURCES

and

Information

The Two-Minute "Tell Me About Yourself" Answer

Nearly every interview starts with a "Tell me about yourself" question. This question typically "kicks-off" the formal portion of the interview.

Because this is the first formal question, it is your opportunity to make a good first impression. While the question is innocent enough, having a well thought-out, prepared answer to this question is critical. A prepared answer prevents you from making the most common error in answering this question— "winging it" and rambling on for a period of time—thus losing the interviewer in the process.

The key to success is having a succinct mini-story to answer this question. The answer should have a logical beginning, middle and end. The answer should not exceed two minutes in length—thus the **Two-Minute "Tell Me About Yourself"** answer**.**

Components of the **Two-Minute "Tell Me About Yourself"** answer include:

1) Introduction/Overview – A sentence or two that summarizes your professional career.
2) Accomplishments – The main component of your **Two-Minute "Tell Me About Yourself"** answer. Here you highlight the key accomplishments of your professional experience.
3) Conclusion – Summarize and conclude the answer.

Since you can almost always expect to have this question asked of you in an interview, this is the one answer that you must have rehearsed and memorized. Having the **Two-Minute "Tell Me About Yourself"** answer committed to memory will help you in other areas of your interview and job search. For example, you can conclude your interview with a version of this answer to wrap up your portion of the interview. Also, having this "infomercial" about yourself can come in handy when you are at networking events.

There are different versions of this question. Other examples include:

- "Why don't you give me a brief overview of your career?"
- "Why should we hire you?"
- "Why do you think you are the best candidate for the job?"

The Two-Minute "Tell Me About Yourself" Answer– Example

Here is my personal example of the **Two-Minute "Tell Me About Yourself"** answer:

"I am a 20-year Sales and Sales Management professional. I started my career in entry level sales and eventually worked my way up to Major Account sales positions. For the past 13 years I have held sales management and leadership positions. I have overseen a variety of sales teams, including multi-location sales teams and a start-up sales operation. In my current position, I oversee the sales effort for a highly-consultative sales team.

I have been a consistent sales and revenue producer in all my positions. Some of my individual sales accomplishments include being recognized as a top-sales performer on several occasions. I once was recognized as the top individual sales producer for a Fortune 500 company. As a Sales Manager, I have consistently produced a high level of sales results. In my current position, I have been a Chairman's Club winner 4 times for outstanding sales and sales management performance.

I consider sales to be a professional skill that can be developed. I think of myself as a student of sales and business in general. I strive to continually develop my professional skills. In addition to constantly reading books on sales and general business topics, I have an MBA from St. Thomas University.

My strengths and skills include sales planning and forecasting, sales training and a high-level grasp of the consultative sales process."

Note that the first paragraph is a high-level overview of my professional career. In the next paragraph, I highlight specific accomplishments from the various positions I have held. Finally, I summarize with some of the specific skills I believe would be valuable to the potential employer.

The Two-Minute "Tell Me About Yourself" Answer – Exercise

Use the following format to create your **Two-Minute "Tell Me About Yourself"** answer

Introduction:

_____

_____

_____

Accomplishments:

_____

_____

_____

_____

_____

_____

_____

Summary:

_____

_____

_____

_____

Once you have composed your **Two-Minute "Tell Me About Yourself"** answer, make sure you rehearse until you have it memorized and can recite it conversationally. Be sure that your answer does *not* exceed two minutes in length.

Questions You Should Ask in the Interview

Once the interviewer has asked all the questions she has, you will typically be asked if you have any questions. This is a very important part of the interview process—and one that many job applicants do not handle well. One of the most commonly cited pet peeves that interviewers have of candidates is that they do not come prepared with good questions, or worse yet—have no questions at all!

When given the opportunity to ask questions during the interview, you are in a position to accomplish three key goals:

1) Differentiate yourself from other applicants vying for the position.
2) Show that you are genuinely interested in the position.
3) Help you understand if this is really a position that you are interested in accepting.

Also, the type of questions you ask will enable you to demonstrate that you have researched the company in advance of the interview. This will help the interviewer see how well you have prepared.

Questions to ask the interviewer fall into into three categories:

1) Questions about the interviewer.
2) Questions about the position.
3) Questions about the company/industry.

Once you have your questions prepared, type them up and bring them along to the interview. This way you will have them available in an easy-to-read format.

START Method for Acing Job Interview Questions Workbook

Questions to Ask the Interviewer

- How did you come to work for this organization?
- What was your background prior to working for this company?
- What attracted you to join this company?
- What do you like most about working for this company?
- How long have you worked for this company?
- In addition to your current role, what other positions have you held within the organization?

Questions to Ask About the Position

- Why is this position available?
- Is this a newly created position? How long has the position been open?
- Who will be my supervisor?
- Describe the typical responsibilities of the position.
- What are the unique challenges of the position?
- What does the initial training program for this position look like?
- Describe the opportunities for professional development and promotion within the organization.
- What are the immediate projects and assignments that I will be working on?
- Which members of the organization will I be working with?
- Describe the ideal candidate for the position.

Questions to Ask About the Company/Industry

- Can you describe the culture and philosophy of the company?
- What are some of the key initiatives that the company is looking to undertake?
- What are some of the greatest opportunities that you anticipate for the company?
- What is the biggest challenge faced by the organization at this time?
- Who are your biggest competitors?
- What do you see as your key differentiators from the competition?
- What are some industry trends that you see?

Interview DO's

- Dress appropriately for the company or industry. If you are unsure, it is better to err on the side of conservative dress.
- Confirm the time and location of your interview.
- Make sure you know how to get to your interview. You may want to do a test drive to the location or use an online tool such as MapQuest or Google Maps to map out interview location.
- Arrive 10 – 15 minutes early for the interview.
- Treat everyone you meet at the company with courtesy and respect.
- Have a firm handshake and a smile.
- Whenever possible, obtain a business card from everyone you meet in the interview. If a business card is not available, ask for the correct spelling of their name and contact information.
- Maintain good body posture and eye contact during the interview.
- If there are forms or applications that you have been asked to complete prior to the interview, make sure you have done so and bring them to your interview.
- Have a nice portfolio and pen to take notes.
- Always tell the truth.
- Bring a prepared list of questions to ask.
- Write or email a thank you note to everyone you met as soon as possible after the interview.
- Bring extra copies of your resume and have a list of references with you should you be asked for them.
- Bring examples of your previous work, or forms of recognition you have received (if applicable).
- Make sure you have researched the company as well as you can prior to the interview.
- At the close of the interview, make sure you confirm what the next steps are in the interview process. Ask permission to follow up on a specific date.
- Remember to thank the interviewer at the end of the interview.
- If you do not understand a question asked of you in the interview, ask for clarification.
- Take a moment before you answer a question to collect your thoughts – but not too long.
- Be positive during the interview. Avoid disparaging comments about previous employers.
- After the interview is over, review your written and mental notes to assess what went well in the interview. Identify what you could do better in future interviews.

Interview DON'TS

- Don't be late for your interview (but don't be too early either).
- Ladies – don't wear too much perfume. Don't put your purse on the table or desk.
- Men – be careful not to wear too much cologne. Place your brief case on the floor.
- Do not chew gum during the interview.
- Do not smoke prior to the interview. Avoid smelling like smoke.
- Make sure your cell phone is turned off. Better yet, do not bring it to the interview. Of course, do not answer any phone calls while in the interview.
- Don't bring food or drink to the interview.
- Do not bring up the topic of salary, benefits, vacation policy, etc. Let the interviewer bring up this topic.
- Do not make it seem that the geographic location of the job is important.
- Avoid saying anything negative about previous employers or supervisors.
- Do not make excuses for any setbacks you have had in your career.
- Don't brag too much about your background and accomplishments.
- Don't bring up controversial topics – avoid discussions about politics or religion.
- Avoid telling jokes, though you can keep a sense of humor.
- Don't talk too fast - try to keep your nerves under control.
- Avoid acting as if you desperately need this job.
- Don't let your frustrations show if you feel the interview is not going the way you had expected.
- Avoid discussing personal or family issues.
- Do not interrupt the interviewer. Make sure you let him finish his questions.
- Don't have pictures or personal information that may not be flattering to you on social media websites.

Links & Resources – Interview and Job Search Resources

www.harveymackay.com – Great source of tools for job seekers.

www.acetheinterview.com – Nice collection of cover letter and resume examples.

www.interviewup.com – An interactive site where you can ask specific questions.

www.theladder.com – A job listing site for high-end positions and includes many job-seeker tools.

www.careerbuilder.com – A massive job listing sites that includes plenty of links to interview advice.

www.hotjobs.com – A job listing site that contains a specific career tools tab.

www.interviewbest.com – A site specifically dedicated to interviewing resources.

www.monster.com – Similar to career builder in the types of resources available.

www.quintcareers.com – Has a nice "career toolkit" link.

www.jobdig.com – A vast collection of articles covering all phases of the job search.

www.best-job-interview.com – Another site dedicated to interviewing resources.

www.asktheheadhunter.com – Resources from the perspective of a professional recruiter.

www.wordking.com – Primarily a resume resource site with links to interviewing resources.

www.jobsearch.about.com – Sign up for their job seekers newsletter.

www.saicareers.com – A comprehensive job seekers website.

www.collegegrad.com – A site catering to new college graduate job seekers.

www.jobinterviewquestions.org – A comprehensive listing of potential interview questions.

www.indeed.com – A meta-search engine for job listings.

www.about.com – Go to the 'careers' channel.

Links & Resources – People, Company and Industry Research

'Take the Cold Out of Cold Calling' (Web Search Secrets) – by Sam Richter. A must-buy book. Do not let the title fool you. This book is an indispensable guide on how to use the internet to access information on industries, companies and people that will help you with research during your job search and interview preparation.

www.samrichter.com – Sam Richter's website.

www.hoovers.com – Company research. Some resources are subscription based.

www.manta.com – Company research. This website is free.

www.portfolio.com – Access data on company information.

www.guidestar.com – Good resource to research non-profit organizations.

www.allbusiness.com – Look for articles and news releases on companies.

www.bizjournals.com – Search for company news and articles.

www.mool.com – Search newspaper, magazines and websites for company information.

www.linkedin.com – Career networking site that includes individual professional profiles, career-based networking groups, job posting and company profiles.

www.newslink.com – Research if a person or company has been mentioned in the local newspaper.

www.twitter.com – See what people are saying, and what is being said about them. Includes job postings.

www.bls.gov –Access the "jobseekers" link for comprehensive list of career guides by industry.

www.asaecenter.org – The Association of Associations. Full of industry information and facts.

www.publist.com – A database of articles collected from a variety of sources.

www.blogsearch.google.com – See if companies/people with whom you are meeting are mentioned in blogs.

Next Steps

Once you have a good set of START answers, practice reciting them out loud. First, work on getting comfortable answering the questions individually. Do not try to memorize your answers verbatim. This is virtually impossible to do—and will only make you appear "scripted" during an interview. Rather, try to have the essence of at least eight START answers in your mind that you can use interchangeably for a variety of interview questions.

A very useful exercise is to set up a mock interview to practice answering questions in an interview environment. You might have a spouse or good friend who is willing to help. Hopefully she can give you feedback on how well you answered the questions and how you might improve your interview skills.

If you really want to be as prepared as possible for your upcoming interviews, I recommend you seek the services of a professional interview coach. He can offer you a level of feedback and constructive criticism that others cannot provide. A professional interview coach has the background and focus to help you be as prepared as possible for your interviews.

If you do an internet search for a professional interview coach, you can identify several potential resources. Read about the methodology of each to determine the specific coaching style that best suits your needs.

Good Luck!

Kurt Thompson – The Interview Pro

www.theinterviewpro.com

Acknowledgments

I would like to thank the following individuals for supporting me during this project:

Katie Murphy – For her invaluable editing and proofreading help.

Sam Richter – For his business advice and mentorship.

Tim McGlinch and Molly Murphy-Valker – For agreeing to be 'guinea pigs' while I refined my START program.

Jane Fust DeBruzzi and Jill DuRose – For being my first paying customers.

Michael Berger – For his friendship and business advice.

Maggie Sainio – For helping create the START answers.

Andrea Boecker – Additional proofreading.

Ward Thompson – My brother. I appreciate all the free technical support and computer advice.

Chuck – More editing and proofreading.

Janet Fine – Even more editing and proofreading.

Robert Pollack – For helping me see that it is possible to publish one's own book.

Chad Nilsson – For letting me see the possibilities.

Mari Taffe – My wife. For everything.